JUAN'S JOURNEY

BY CAROL HERRERA
ILLUSTRATED BY CYNTHIA SEARS

PEARSON

Scott
Foresman

Editorial Offices: Glenview, Illinois • Parsippany, New Jersey • New York, New York
Sales Offices: Needham, Massachusetts • Duluth, Georgia • Glenview, Illinois
Coppell, Texas • Ontario, California • Mesa, Arizona

Every effort has been made to secure permission and provide appropriate credit for photographic material. The publisher deeply regrets any omission and pledges to correct errors called to its attention in subsequent editions.

Unless otherwise acknowledged, all photographs are the property of Scott Foresman, a division of Pearson Education.

Photo locators denoted as follows: Top (T), Center (C), Bottom (B), Left (L), Right (R), Background (Bkgd)

Illustrations by Cynthia Sears

ISBN: 0-328-13517-8

5 6 7 8 9 10 V0G1 14 13 12 11 10 09 08 07

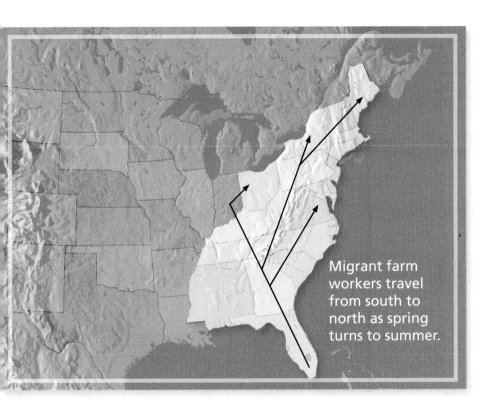

Migrant farm workers travel from south to north as spring turns to summer.

The rain was coming down hard the day the Garcia family packed their stuff into their old station wagon and headed north. It was mid-June. The Garcias had been in Georgia since April. There they had worked on a farm picking tomatoes and peppers. The harvest was now over. It was time for the Garcias to move on to the next job.

Juan and his two little sisters were used to moving a lot. Their parents were migrant farmworkers. They traveled around the country following the crops as they came into season. They picked cucumbers in South Carolina and cabbages in North Carolina. In Virginia they would pick apples until the apple season ended in October. Then they would travel back south to Florida. There Juan would go to school for part of the year.

3

The Garcias had to set up a new home every time they moved. Sometimes home was a tiny trailer owned by the person who ran the farm. Other times home was the tent that the Garcias kept in their car.

Juan worked hard when the family arrived at each new farm. He unloaded the car as quickly as he could. While he did he would think to himself, *Maybe this time we could stay.* But the dream had never become reality.

Juan was twelve now. He wished that he belonged somewhere. He wished something belonged to him. A pet would help. Juan longed for a dog. But his parents always said no. It was too hard to travel with animals. And dogs were expensive to feed.

Juan's parents were named Manuel and Teresa. During the harvest season they went looking for jobs. They would learn which farmers in an area were hiring. Then they would ask them for work.

This season, Manuel and Teresa were doing things differently. They had agreed to work for a crew leader. The crew leader wasn't a farm owner. He wasn't a farmworker. Instead, he was a middleman. He found jobs for farmworkers and set up their harvest schedules. He would help them find places to live. The crew leader also arranged rides to work for farmworkers who needed them. In return, he kept part of each worker's pay.

Manuel was wary about the deal. He worried that the crew leader would take too much of his pay. He didn't want to give money to someone who didn't work with him.

But Manuel didn't have a choice. Bad weather had ruined many of the crops. Because of that there was less work than usual. Unsure of what to do, Manuel and Teresa had agreed to sign on with a crew leader. The crew leader had promised them jobs picking strawberries in Cayuga County, New York. That's where the Garcias were headed.

The rain fell against the car windows. Juan watched it streak down in different directions. Everyone was quiet. His sisters, Maria and Rosa, had both fallen asleep. Even his mother seemed to be dozing. Juan worried about his mother. She frequently complained of being tired. But she said she couldn't sleep. Perhaps it was worry about the future that kept his mother awake.

Juan's mother had been too tired to work recently. In the past she had brought Juan's sisters into the fields with her. Maria was five years old. She had already become a good babysitter for Rosa. Rosa was just two. Maria knew what games Rosa liked to play. The one where Maria had Rosa find a caterpillar was Rosa's favorite. Juan felt sad knowing that his sisters hadn't had a chance to play the game recently.

Juan kept watching his mother. He thought of all the things he would like to do for her when he was older. He would buy her a house so she and his father would never have to move again. He would buy one right next door for himself. He would make sure his parents had a car that always worked. It would be a red one. Red was his mother's favorite color.

Juan's mother stretched and opened her eyes. She noticed that Juan was watching her again. *His face is sad and serious,* she thought. *It makes him look much older than twelve.* She smiled at her son.

"What were you thinking about?" Juan's mother asked.

"Strawberries," said Juan. "Millions of strawberries–all the strawberries I can pick in Cayuga County."

Juan planned to join his father in the fields when they got to New York. Now that he was twelve, the law allowed him to work as a crop picker. Juan was determined to help his family by earning some money. Strawberries, plump and plentiful, were crowding the fields in Cayuga. Juan was sure he could pick mountains of them.

There was only one thing that worried him. It was the crew leader, Mr. Spike. Juan was dreading the idea of working for him. He sensed his father was too. Even the man's name made Juan shiver.

The Garcias finally reached Cayuga County. They were anxious to get to the farm and their new home. Manuel pulled a crumpled map from his pocket. It had been sketched and sent in the mail by Mr. Spike. The map showed the way to the camp the Garcias would be sharing with other farmworker families.

Soon the Garcias arrived at their new home. It was half of a sagging, one-story house. The Garcias' side had just one room and a tiny kitchen.

Juan, as always, ran around doing everything he could to help his family get settled. He was reaching into the car to haul out the last box when he heard someone behind him say in a gruff voice, "You with the Garcias?"

Juan turned. Standing over him was a tall man with thick limbs. His hands looked powerful. The fingers, however, were short, fat, and pointed at the end. They reminded Juan of bird's claws.

"I'm Mr. Spike. If you're the Garcia boy, you had better be at the field by sunrise. Tell your dad too." He stalked off slowly. His heavy boots left puffs of dust after each step.

Juan and Manuel arrived at the strawberry fields at sunrise the next morning. For the rest of the week they picked berries. They picked so many that Juan lost track of how many he had placed in his picker's bucket.

It was hot in the fields. All they had to drink was the water they had brought with them. Juan spilled his one day when his bottle slipped from his hands after he unscrewed the top. Manuel shared what he had left with his son. But it wasn't nearly enough for either of them.

Juan was looking forward to one thing: the money he and his father would receive at the end of the week. He was sure the pay would be good, given how many berries they had picked. Manuel was also confident that the pay would be good. He was keeping count of what they were owed.

Payday came. Mr. Spike told the workers to meet him at his truck after they had hauled in their last load of berries. He said he would give them their paychecks then.

The workers gathered round him in the dusk when they finished. They were tired and dirty. Mr. Spike held a fistful of checks. One by one he handed them out. It was nearly dark, making it hard to read the numbers on the checks. Most of the workers put their checks in their pockets and headed home.

Manuel peered at his check closely. He still didn't trust Mr. Spike. Just as he had feared, something was wrong. *This couldn't be the right amount,* he thought. *Not for all the berries I have picked!* It should have been at least fifty dollars more. Mr. Spike was climbing into his truck when Manuel approached him.

"Excuse me, Mr. Spike. There's a mistake on my check," said Manuel. "It's short by about fifty dollars."

Mr. Spike glared down at him from his seat in the cab. He took Manuel's words as a sign of disrespect. But the truth was that he had been cheating the workers out of some of their pay for a while. He figured most would never notice. If they did, they wouldn't have the nerve to say anything. Lately, Mr. Spike had been stealing even more. It had been easy, until now.

"You accusing me of something?" Mr. Spike snapped at Manuel. "Maybe you can't read. Maybe you can't add. Maybe you should just go home." He revved the engine hard. "Get out of my way," he said.

Manuel stood his ground. "I need my money," he said.

Mr. Spike put the truck into reverse. It lurched back.

"Move!" he roared. With a squeal of tires, Mr. Spike shifted into forward and raced by Manuel. Just then, Manuel saw a shadow emerge from the bushes near where they were standing. It was a little dog. It hobbled slowly into the path of the truck. Mr. Spike swerved wildly, just missing the dog. He then sped off down the road.

Manuel let out a deep sigh. He knew he'd never get the missing fifty dollars. He also knew he wouldn't work for a crook, no matter how badly he needed a job. Tomorrow he would look for a new one.

"Let's go," Manuel said to Juan, who had been standing beside him the entire time. Manuel turned to walk back home. His son followed. But then Juan heard something. A soft whimpering sound was coming from the bushes.

"Dad, I can hear that dog crying. I think he's hurt," said Juan. "We've got to help him."

Manuel nodded. He suddenly felt more tired than ever. Mr. Spike had robbed him of his money, and now there was this hurt dog. But he couldn't ignore a suffering animal. Juan couldn't either.

"Go get him," said Manuel.

Juan waded into the bushes and found the dog. He was licking his leg. It looked broken. Juan scooped the dog up in his arms. He had a pointy nose and a bushy tail. Juan knew the dog was a stray because he didn't have a collar.

Manuel and Juan made a splint for the dog's leg using some rags and a bit of wood. Juan named the dog Silver.

Later that night, Manuel came to talk to his son. "Your mother and I agreed you can keep the dog," he said. "But you have to feed and take care of him. Promise?"

"Promise!" Juan said. At last, he had something that belonged to him!

Juan awoke in the morning with the sun streaming into the tiny house. His father was gone. Silver lay wrapped in a tight little cocoon of blankets at the foot of Juan's bed. Juan jumped up, confused.

"Where's Dad?" he asked. "What about Mr. Spike?"

"Don't worry," said his mother. Manuel had told her about what had happened with Mr. Spike. "Dad's gone to look for work on a different farm. He'll find something. You saw all the farms we passed on the way here."

Manuel returned late in the afternoon. He had driven all over Cayuga County.

"There's not much work out there," said Manuel, sinking into a chair. "But there are a few days of picking on the far side of the county. I think we should pack up and try over there. I'll feel relieved the sooner we get away from that crook Mr. Spike."

Juan's mother had already started filling boxes with their things. "Why not go now?" she said. Manuel thought about it. "You're right," he agreed. "We might as well get moving."

Together, they finished packing, and moved their things to the car. *Maybe this time we'll be able to stay*, Juan thought. The Garcias finished packing and drove off into the gathering darkness.

Learning While Moving: A Balancing Act

As you might have guessed, the children of migrant farmworkers can have a hard time trying to learn at school. Their families move frequently, going from one farm job to the next. The children switch schools just as frequently. This can interrupt learning and cause the children to fall behind on their school work.

To address the problem, some school districts have created special programs to improve education for migrant families. These programs offer extra help to both students and parents who are learning how to read. Other programs may provide school supplies, uniforms, and bus passes.

Teachers in one Florida county turned to the Internet to help their migrant farmworker students. They created online learning programs for each child. The programs give teachers nationwide the ability to review the progress each child has made, no matter what state the families move to.

A child of a migrant farmworker studies at a mobile school